# Let's Try It Out in the Water

WITHDRAWN

## Hands-On Early-Learning Science Activities

by **Seymour Simon** and **Nicole Fauteux**

illustrated by **Doug Cushman**

Aladdin Paperbacks

New York    London    Toronto    Sydney    Singapore

# Note to Parents, Teachers, and Child-Care Providers

In *Let's Try It Out in the Water,* children will learn about buoyancy. They will be able to observe that objects that are heavier than an equal volume of water sink, and objects that are lighter than an equal volume of water float. They will also develop an appreciation of the relative capacity of containers and learn a method for comparing their volumes. This will help them draw conclusions about why some things sink and others float.

Through a series of experiments and other activities derived from play, children will acquire a basic understanding of the following concepts:

- *It is difficult to predict a container's capacity by looking at it.*
- *We can use water to compare the relative volumes of containers.*
- *An object that contains air will float because air is lighter than water.*
- *The greater an object's surface area, the more likely it is to float.*

The activities described in this book use these readily available materials:
- *water in a bathtub, sink, water table, or wading pool*
- *plastic bottles and containers*
- *other unbreakable, waterproof objects and toys*
- *a sheet of aluminum foil*
- *turkey baster or water pistol*

Encourage your children to use their imaginations in collecting the waterproof objects and containers. Their learning will increase as the variety of their selections increases.

First Aladdin Paperbacks edition July 2003

Text copyright © 2001 by Seymour Simon and Nicole Fauteux
Illustrations copyright © by 2001 Doug Cushman

ALADDIN PAPERBACKS
An imprint of Simon & Schuster
Children's Publishing Division
1230 Avenue of the Americas
New York, NY 10020

Also available in a Simon & Schuster Books for Young Readers hardcover edition.
Designed by Anahid Hamparian
The text of this book was set in 19-point New Baskerville.

Manufactured in China
2  4  6  8  10  9  7  5  3  1

The Library of Congress has cataloged the hardcover edition as follows:
Simon, Seymour.
Let's try it out in the water / by Seymour Simon and Nicole Fauteux.
p. cm.
Summary: Presents simple activities and experiments that demonstrate buoyancy by observing why some things sink and others float in water.
ISBN 0-689-82919-1 (hc.)
1. Floating bodies Experiments—Juvenile literature [1. Floating bodies Experiments. 2. Water Experiments. 3. Experiments.] I. Fauteux, Nicole. II. Title
QC147.5.S56 2000      99-20371
532'.25—dc21      CIP
ISBN 0-689-86012-9 (pbk.)

To Joyce and our wonderful grandkids:
Joel, Benjamin, Chloe, and Jeremy.   —S. S.

To Ed Shore, an extraordinary teacher,
who first taught me the value of trying it out.
And thanks to Martha Hummer and her morning
kindergartners at Olde Creek Elementary School
for trying these activities out.   —N. F.

Imagine you are standing on a sandy beach looking out at the ocean. Children run and jump in the surf. Swimmers bob in the waves. Birds skirt the water's edge in search of a meal.

Farther out small boats cruise past. Huge tanker ships look like bathtub toys on the distant horizon. Everything looks small compared to the ocean.

Water stretches out in front of you as far as you can see.

Can you guess how much water is in the ocean? Probably not.

But can you guess how much water is in something smaller?

## Let's try it out.

Find a large plastic container, like a milk jug, a pitcher, or a soda bottle. Guess how many containers of water it will take to fill your bathtub or wading pool—or the sink or water table at your school. Then start filling. Is your guess correct?

Were you surprised by how much water the bathtub holds? Then this next activity may surprise you too.

Collect some empty plastic containers, like pitchers, yogurt containers, margarine tubs, plastic cups, and ketchup or shampoo bottles. Make sure your containers are different shapes and sizes.

Put your tallest container next to your widest one. Which do you think will hold more water?

## Let's try it out.

Fill the tall container with water and pour it into the wide container. Does the water spill over the sides, or do you need to add more water in order to fill it completely?

See if you and your friends can line up the empty containers from the one that you think holds the least water to the one that holds the most. When you're finished, use a small plastic cup to fill them with water.

Count the number of cups of water it takes to fill each container. Did you place them in the right order?

When containers are all the same shape, it's easy to line them up in size order. But when some are wide, some are narrow, some tall and some short, it can be hard to tell which containers hold more liquid and which ones hold less by looking at them.

Let's imagine you are back at the ocean, playing at the water's edge. You dig a beach pebble out of the wet sand. You throw it as far as you can and watch it splash. Then it disappears. The pebble sinks to the sandy bottom.

Now you look out at the horizon and see a large ocean liner. It has thousands of people onboard, many restaurants, and even a swimming pool. It weighs more than every person on your whole street put together. But the ocean liner is **not** sinking. It is floating on the water.

Let's find out why some things sink and some things float.

For this activity you'll need odds and ends from around the house, including bath toys, plastic balls and animals, and plastic containers—anything that won't be damaged if it gets wet. Make sure that the objects you choose aren't breakable.

You will also need a sheet of aluminum foil for later.

Pick up two of the objects you collected. Put one on the palm of each hand.

Which is heavier? Which is lighter? Which do you think will sink? Which do you think will float?

## Let's try it out.

Return to the bathtub or water table that you filled. If you filled
a wading pool and you feel like getting wet, climb in!

Use your hands to weigh each of the objects you collected.
Then drop them in the water one at a time.

What sinks? What floats? Do heavy things always sink? Do light things always float?

Leave the objects in the water as you add more things. Do "floaters" sometimes sink? Do "sinkers" sometimes rise?

Find something small that sinks, like a spoon or several coins. Next, take a sheet of aluminum foil and fold up the edges to make a boat.

Float your boat on the water's surface. What do you think will happen when you place your "sinkers" on top? Try it out.

Are you surprised? The sinkers do not weigh any less than they did before. They are able to float because the aluminum foil spreads their weight over more of the surface.

Your aluminum foil boat floats very well, but is it unsinkable? Try this: Pick it up and put it back in the water on its side. What happens when its weight rests on a narrow strip of the water instead of a wider area? Does it sink or float?

Here's another way to sink your aluminum foil boat. Scrunch up the sides so that the bottom of the boat gets smaller. Then place your boat on the water again with the sinkers on top. If your boat **still** floats, fold the sides of the boat over the top of your sinkers and scrunch them together as tightly as you can. When your boat is small enough, it will quickly sink to the bottom.

Next time you are in a swimming pool or pond, you can try this with your own body. (If you don't know how to swim, you will need a grown-up to help you.)

Stretch out your arms and legs, then lean back as far as you can.

Does the water hold you up? If it does, you are floating.

Now stand up straight. Can you float on top of the water in this position? No. Your feet sink to the bottom.

Here are some fun things to do with your friends.

Pretend you are running a shipping business. Choose something that floats to use as your barge. Place your "goods" on it and send it upriver (to the other end of the tub or water table). Your friend will unload it, place some new goods on the barge, and send it back. See who can safely deliver the most goods without losing any in the river.

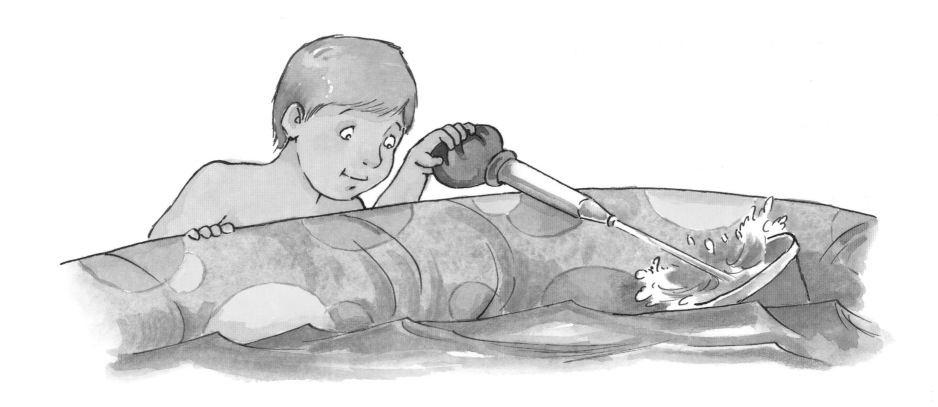

What would happen if one of your boats sprang a leak?

Try this: Choose an empty container that will float on the water. Then fill up a turkey baster or a water pistol. Squirt water into the container a little at a time. It will start to fill up the way a leaky boat does. How long can it stay afloat? How quickly can you make it sink?

You can also host a pretend party in your tub. Pour some water into a plastic cup and place it on top of a small cookie sheet or a plastic dinner plate. How many friends can you serve using the same tray? How many cups of water can your tray hold before it sinks?

Find two empty plastic bottles that are about the same size. Fill one with water, then tightly cap them both.

Hold one bottle in each hand. Which weighs more: the bottle with water inside, or the empty bottle?

Drop the lighter bottle in the water. Now push it to the bottom of the tub and let go. It keeps floating up, doesn't it? The bottle floats because there is air in it and air is lighter than water.

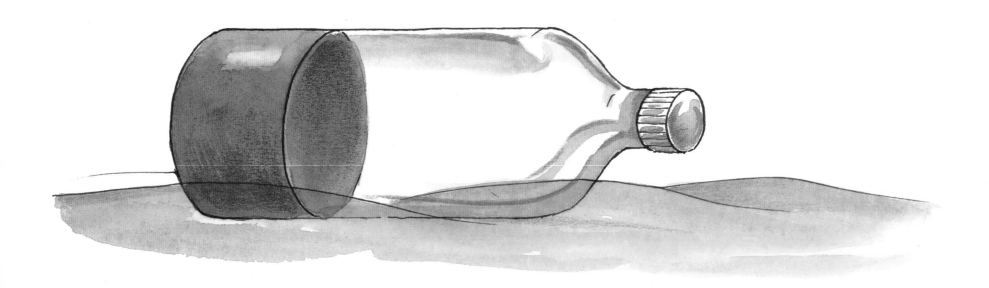

Now put the bottle of water in the tub. Does one end of the
bottle rise to the surface? Can you guess why?

Take the bottle out of the tub and look inside it.

What is in there with the water? You guessed it: air.

Now that you know what sinks and what floats, you and your friends can search for sunken treasure in the bathtub.

Use things that always sink for treasure, things that always float for boats, and things that can do both (like your plastic bottle) to transport your underwater search team.

But watch out. Pirates lurk around every bend. Worse yet, a hurricane is coming. Heavy rains (from your turkey baster or water pistol) could sink your ship. And remember not to get too greedy or the treasure itself may send your ship plummeting to the bottom of the deep.

Good luck on your adventure. Who knows? You might discover something wonderful right in your very own bathtub.

*Let's Try It Out in the Water* is structured so that teachers can present all the activities in a single session. With younger children, teachers may prefer to cover the material in two or three twenty- to thirty-minute sessions over the course of a week. Ideally, the class should be divided into smaller groups so that each child can fully experience each of the activities for himself or herself.

Parents and caregivers may find it more rewarding to use the book in shorter time intervals, pulling it off the shelf to introduce an activity when they find their children already engaged in related play. A bathtub sea battle provides a ready opportunity for teaching children about buoyancy. Or you can add a little science to a backyard pool party by making a game of the container volume activities.

The Let's Try It Out series integrates the scientific method into everyday life by using only safe, readily available materials and by modeling the experiments it presents on play. The books encourage children to use their body and their senses to explore their surroundings.

Parents and teachers can use these books to help children make observations in the course of their play, recognize the significance of these observations, and organize them in such a way that children can draw some preliminary conclusions about how things work in the fascinating world around them.

Parents and teachers should not be disturbed if children sometimes draw the wrong conclusions from these activities. Children's cognitive development varies greatly at young ages, and some children may not yet be able to grasp every concept presented. Forcing children to accept your explanation of a phenomenon they cannot understand will undermine your main goals of teaching them to observe carefully, form hypotheses, and test them. Chances are that if you reintroduce a challenging activity six months later, a child will be ready to draw the right conclusion for himself or herself.

You can also use the Internet to find out more about this book and others in the series. Visit our Web site at www.SimonSaysKids.com. We value your suggestions and comments about your experiences using our books with your children.

Seymour Simon
Nicole Fauteux